Flying Colors

Window Entertainment

By Virginia Cabibil Carlson

About the Author

Virginia Cabibil Carlson is a Filipina-American who lives in Minnetonka, Minnesota. She is an elementary school teacher and a nurse by profession. She is an avid bird-lover and enjoys spending time observing and taking pictures of the birds in her backyard. The inspiration for this book was her grandson Laken. She is thrilled that Laken's first word in Filipino was "langgam" which means "bird" in Cebuano, her native tongue.

Dedicated to family especially to Ayla Anatolia, the
newest member

and

In memory of Pa and Ma

Copyright © 2015 by Virginia Cabibil Carlson

ISBN-13: 978-1508726289

ISBN-10: 1508726280

The purpose of this book is fourfold: **First,** it gives children some ideas on how to attract birds to their backyard. **Second**, it helps children identify the birds that commonly visit their backyard. **Third,** it allows children to relate birds' color to the primary and secondary colors on the color wheel. **Lastly**, the book provides worksheets as an activity to illustrate what has been learned. In addition children can do the activity with an adult to encourage bonding time.

A wise old owl sat in an oak,

The more he heard, the less he spoke;

The less he spoke, the more he heard;

Why aren't we all like that wise old bird?

Author: Unknown

Hello! I am the wise owl. Let me tell you about the birds around me. Birds are wonderful guests. You can encourage them to visit. Please provide a safe environment for them. Remember, the use of chemicals is not only harmful to lakes, rivers and streams, it also harms birds when they eat poisoned worms, insects, plants and flowers.

You can attract birds to your yard by providing food, shelter and water. Beside these basic needs, birds are attracted to moving water. Some of them, like hummingbirds, love to fly in a mist of water. In your yard, the flowering plants, shrubs and fruit trees provide food and places for birds to build their nests. Your garden also helps birds find shelter from predators and harsh weather.

Birds need trees to hide from predators.

You may find these birds in the spring, summer, fall and winter.

The shrubs and bushes in your yard help protect birds from harsh weather like a snow storm. Birds need shelter in all seasons.

Birds need food as well as water to drink.

They need clean water year round.

Some of them will readily accept your offer of

"ready to move in" housing

07/01/2011

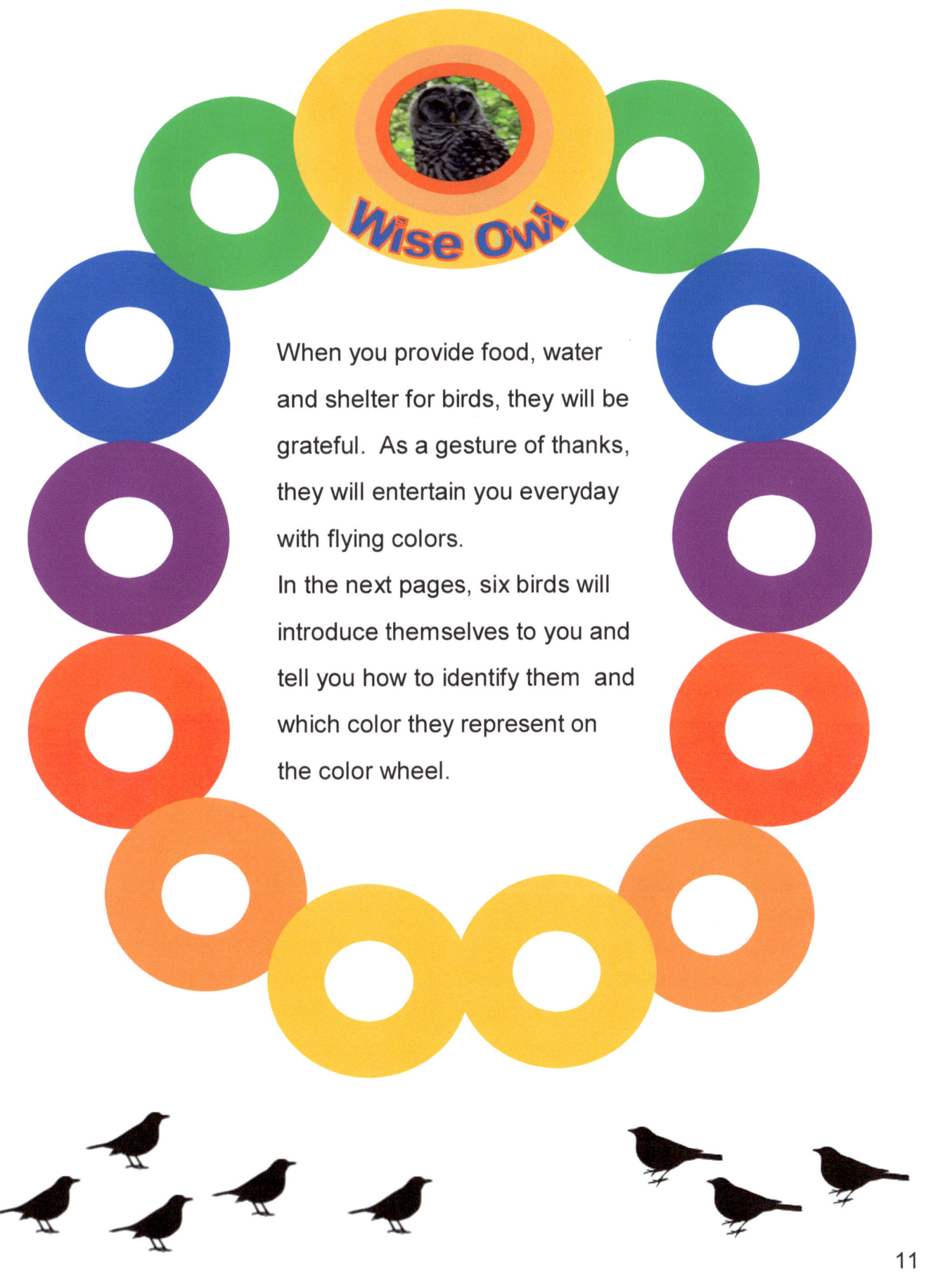

When you provide food, water and shelter for birds, they will be grateful. As a gesture of thanks, they will entertain you everyday with flying colors.

In the next pages, six birds will introduce themselves to you and tell you how to identify them and which color they represent on the color wheel.

Hello!

I am a male American Goldfinch. I visit your yard in the winter, spring, summer and fall. I like Nyger seeds as well as black oil and hulled sunflower seeds.

I am mostly bright yellow with a black cap. I have black and white wings and tail. I am bright yellow because I am the male. A female American Goldfinch is a duller yellow without a black cap. In the winter, I change my feathers to look like a female.

Primary Colors: Yellow, Blue and Red

Yellow is one of the primary colors on the color wheel.

Hello!

I am a male Eastern Bluebird. I visit your yard in the spring and summer. I eat fruit but my favorite food is insects. I especially love mealworms. I will build a nest in your yard if you put up a house for me.

I am mostly blue with a rusty colored breast and white on the belly. I am bright blue because I am the male.

A female Eastern Bluebird is duller blue.

Primary Colors: Yellow , Blue and Red

Blue is one of the primary colors on the color wheel.

Hello!

I am a male Northern Cardinal. I visit your yard in the winter, spring, summer and fall. I like seeds such as striped, black oil or hulled sunflower and safflower seeds.

I am mostly red with a black face and a pink beak.

I am bright red because I am the male. A female Northern Cardinal is brownish red.

Primary Colors: Yellow, Blue and Red.

Red is one of the primary colors on the color wheel.

As a wise owl, I know that many birds have secondary colors. Secondary colors are formed by mixing two primary colors. Let me tell you about the secondary colors. The secondary colors are green, orange, and purple. **Green** is formed by mixing yellow and blue; **Orange** is formed by mixing red and yellow; **Purple** is formed by mixing blue and red.

Secondary Colors: **Orange**, **Green** and **Purple**

Secondary Colors

Hello!

I am a male Baltimore Oriole. I visit your yard in the spring and summer. I like sweets. Grape jelly, orange slices and mealworms are my favorite foods.

I have a bright orange rump and underparts, with a black head, neck and back. I have white and black wings. I am bright orange because I am the male. A female Baltimore Oriole is yellow with an olive colored head. Orange is one of the secondary colors on the color wheel.

Secondary Color—Orange

If you mix yellow and red in equal amounts,
the resulting color is orange.

Hello!

I am a male Purple Finch. I visit your yard in the spring and fall.

I like black oil, striped and hulled sunflower seeds.

I have purplish red color all over my body. I have reddish brown wings

and a black tail. I am mostly purplish red because I am the male.

A female Purple Finch is brown and heavily streaked with a white -

lined eyebrow. Purple is one of the secondary colors on the

color wheel.

Secondary Color—Purple

If you mix red and blue in equal amounts,
the resulting color is purple.

Hello!

I am a male Ruby - Throated Hummingbird. I visit your yard in the spring and summer. I am attracted to colorful tubular flowers. I feed on flower nectar as well as sugared water. I also feed on spiders and insects found around flowers.

My back is fluorescent green and I have a red throat. I am a brighter color because I am the male. A female Ruby -Throated Hummingbird is duller and has a white throat. Green is one of the secondary colors on the color wheel.

Secondary Color—Green

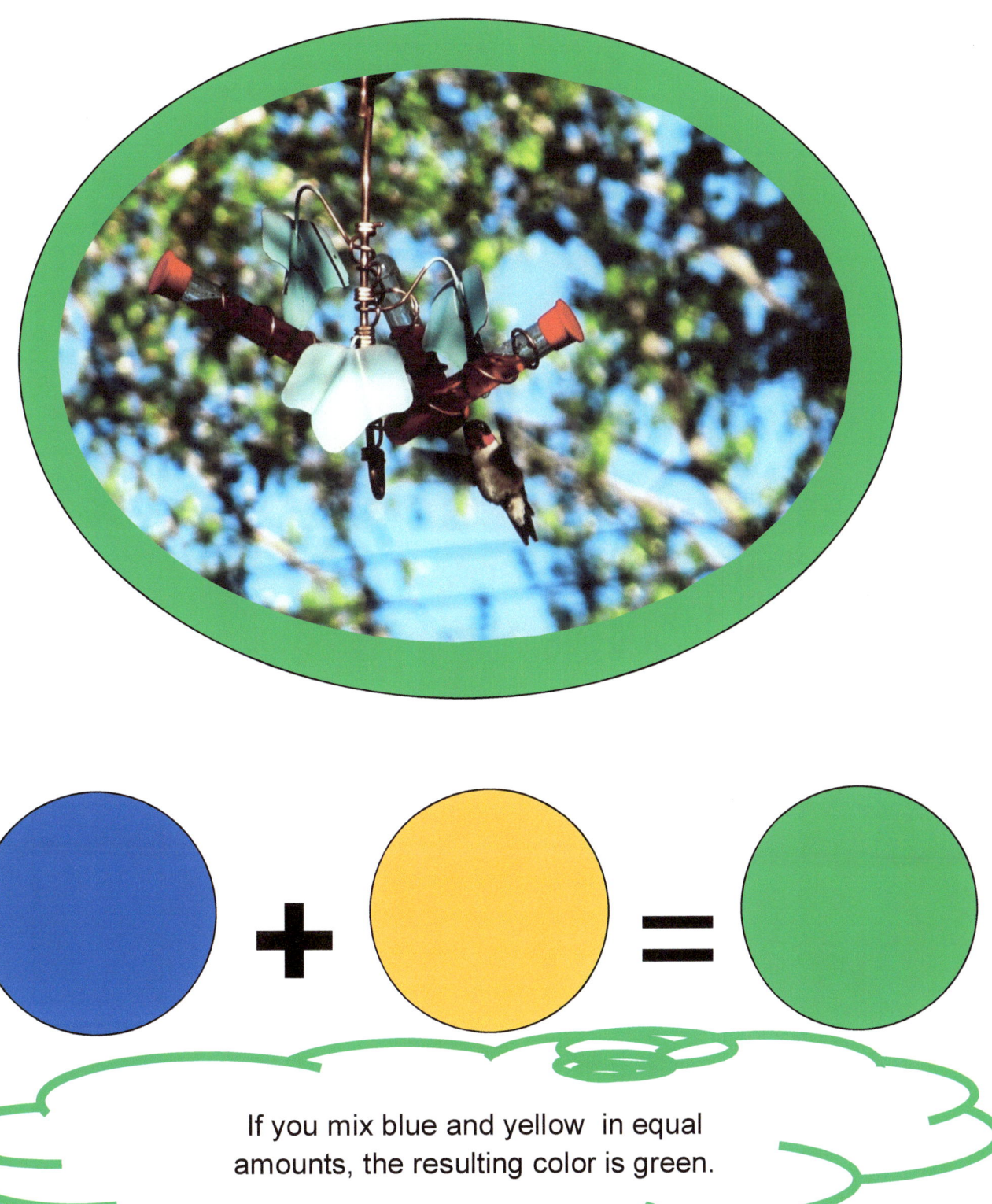

If you mix blue and yellow in equal amounts, the resulting color is green.

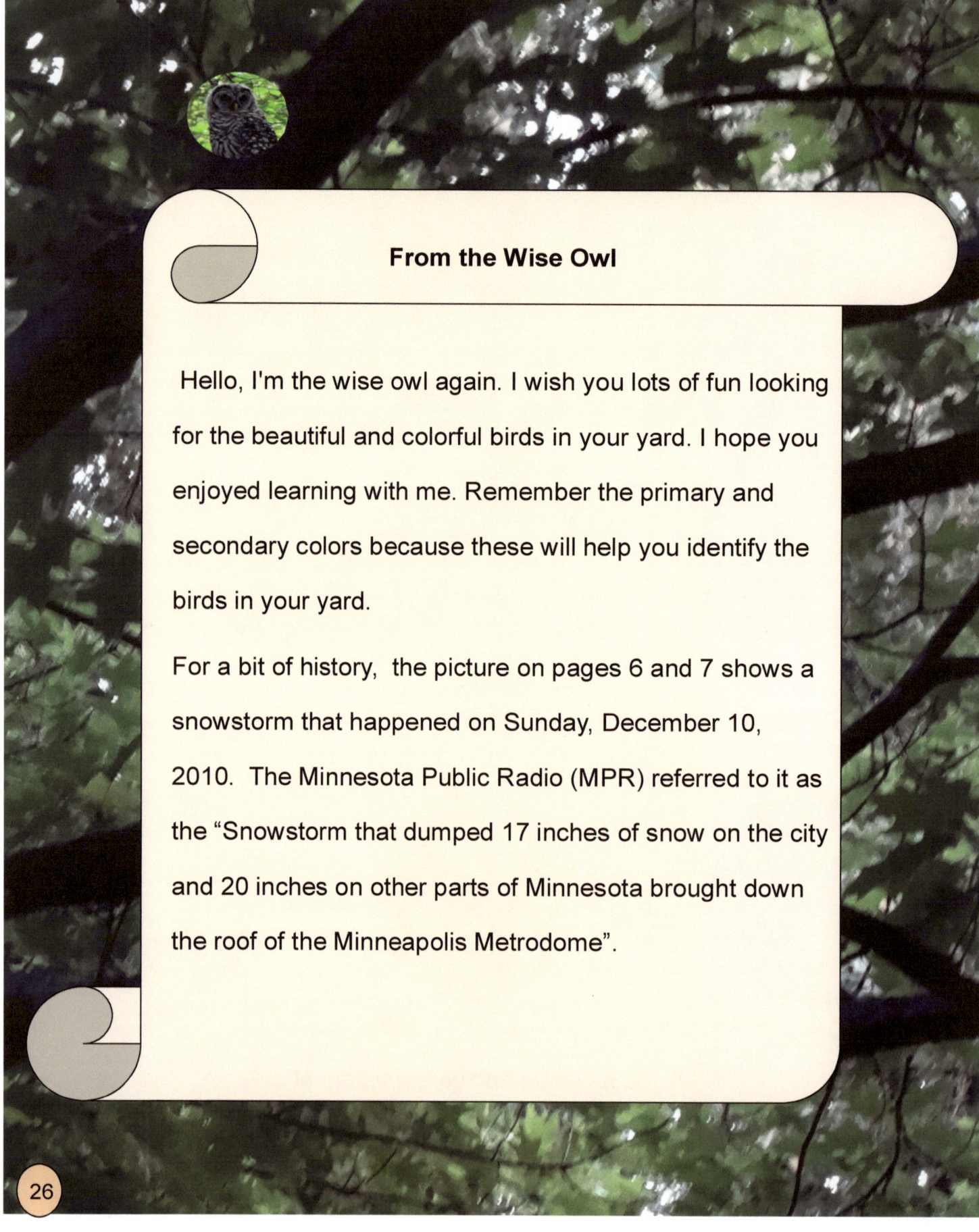

From the Wise Owl

Hello, I'm the wise owl again. I wish you lots of fun looking for the beautiful and colorful birds in your yard. I hope you enjoyed learning with me. Remember the primary and secondary colors because these will help you identify the birds in your yard.

For a bit of history, the picture on pages 6 and 7 shows a snowstorm that happened on Sunday, December 10, 2010. The Minnesota Public Radio (MPR) referred to it as the "Snowstorm that dumped 17 inches of snow on the city and 20 inches on other parts of Minnesota brought down the roof of the Minneapolis Metrodome".

WORKSHEETS

for

ACTIVITIES

The worksheets can be reproduced.

SUGGESTED ACTIVITY
MIXING COLORS

Things needed:

1. Apron - you can use a garbage bag by cutting a hole in the middle on the top part of the garbage bag for the neck and two openings of the sides of the bag for the arms.

2. Table protector - you can use a garbage bag to line your working area.

3. Paints - Red, Blue, Yellow (Make sure you choose paints that are washable and non-toxic).

4. Paint brushes - minimum of 6

5. Small jars with water for rinsing brushes - at least 3

6. Medicine dropper(6) - you can use this to draw paint in equal amounts.

7. Small containers (6) such as bottle caps - you can use the bottle caps to mix the paints.

Instructions:

1. Put an apron on to avoid paint on clothes.

2. Cover the table or the work area where you are mixing colors.

3 Mix two (2) primary colors of your choice in equal amounts by using the medicine dropper. For example: mix red and yellow paints.

Observation

What color is formed when you mix 2 primary colors of equal amounts?

4. Continue to experiment by mixing two (2) different primary colors.

COLORING ACTIVITY

Remember, six birds introduced themselves to you. The following pages are sketches of those birds. You may color one or all of them.

You may reproduce the worksheets if you need more copies to share with friends. You may invite your friends for a coloring activity.

HAVE FUN!

REMEMBER!

The following pages are sketches of birds that represent the primary colors on the color wheel-Yellow, Blue and Red.

Yellow

American

Goldfinch

Yellow

Blue

Eastern

Bluebird

Blue

Red

Northern

Cardinal

Red

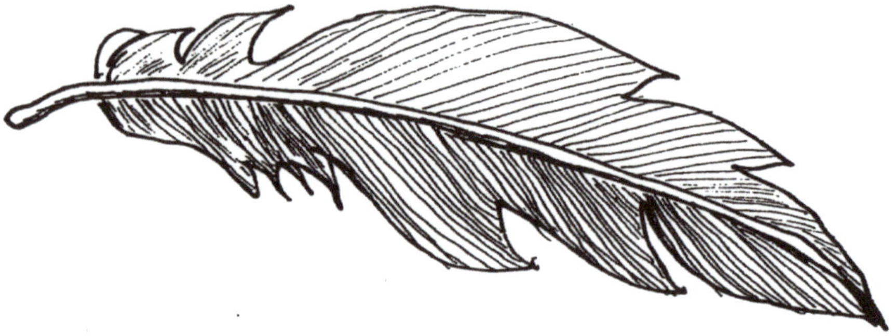

REMEMBER!

The following pages are sketches of birds that represent the secondary colors on the color wheel - orange, purple and green.

Red

Baltimore

Oriole

REMEMBER!

To make the orange of the
Baltimore Oriole, mix red and
yellow together in your
container.

Yellow

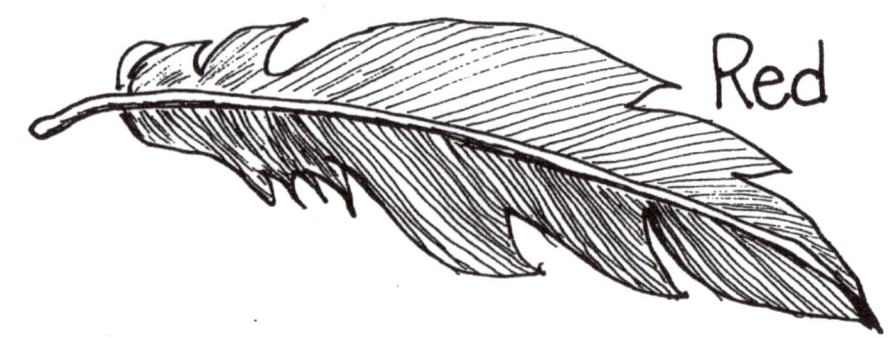

Red

REMEMBER!
To make the purple of the Purple Finch, mix red and blue together in your container.

Purple Finch

Blue

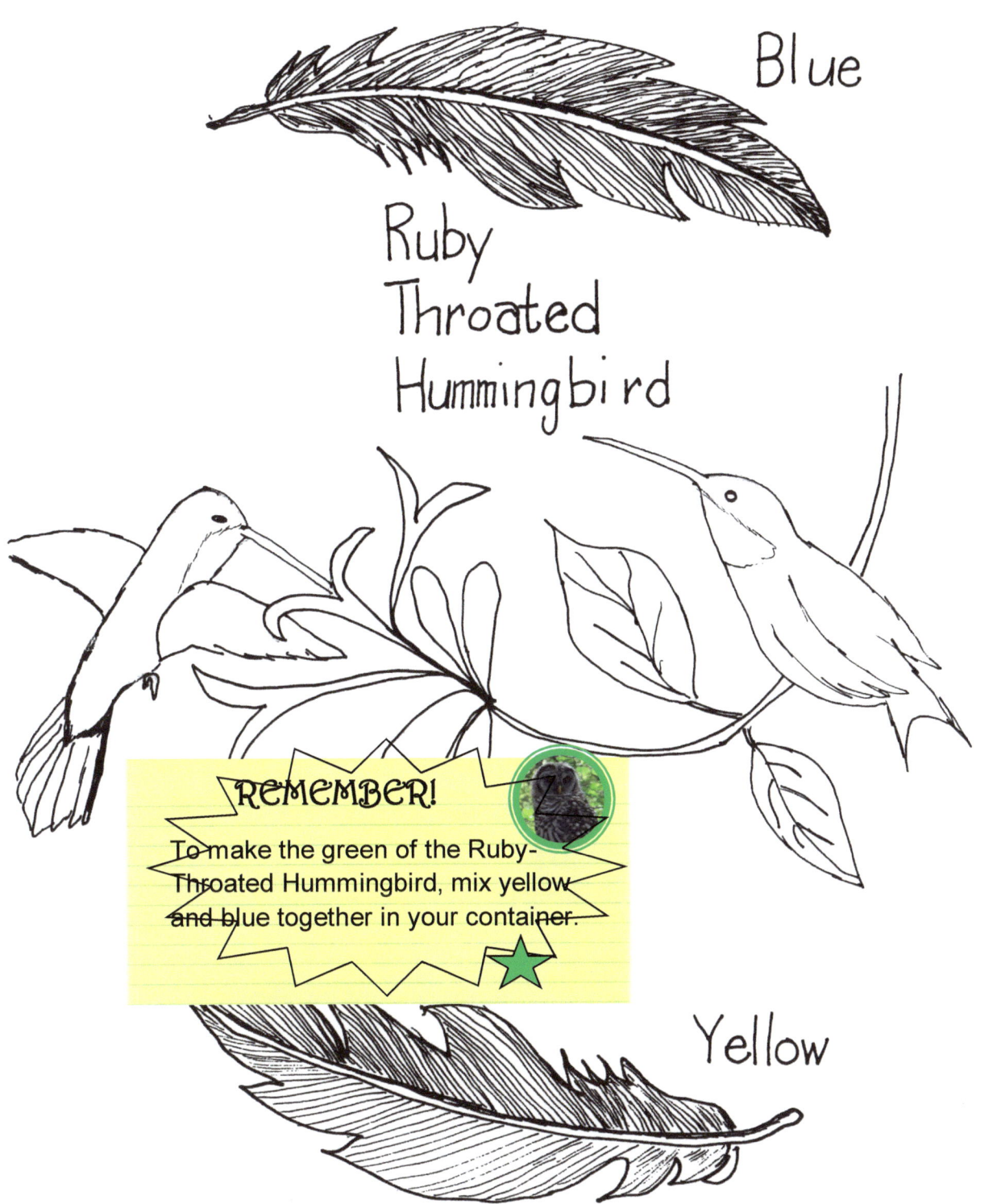

Blue

Ruby
Throated
Hummingbird

REMEMBER!

To make the green of the Ruby-Throated Hummingbird, mix yellow and blue together in your container.

Yellow

Thank You

For taking the time to learn about birds with me.

You learned how to identify birds by knowing the primary and secondary colors on the color wheel. You also learned how to attract birds to your yard.

Your time with me was soooooo precious! I am glad we met each other. Look for me too as you search for birds around you. I will be hooooooting

for you!

Acknowledgment

This book would have not been possible without the contribution of the following:

My husband, Paul, my daughter, Caroline, and my friend, Linda Atwood-Goldetsky for editing.

Thanks also to my son, Chris, who helped me in many ways with projects that helped attract birds to our yard. With his supportive help, I have successfully attracted at least seventy species (70) to our yard some of which are pictured in this book.

A special thanks to Pax Christi Church Environmental Ministry. Because of the program, "**Creating for Solidarity: From St Francis to Pope Francis To You,**" I met parishioners who value the interrelationships of creation and social justice. Through the program, I met Peg Musegades, an elementary school teacher and the illustrator of the activity worksheets.

www.ingramcontent.com/pod-product-compliance
Lightning Source LLC
Chambersburg PA
CBHW041519280526
45792CB00004B/1307